I0488050

SAY WHAT? WHAT'D YOU SAY?

"**Gargantuan Networking** is a must read for anyone desiring to expand his business quickly. Richard, with his broad business acumen and experience, provides a deeper understanding of all aspects of business. Numerous actionable examples highlight today's best business practices for success. Thank you, Richard, for your noteworthy insights!"

~ Gabriele Blankenship, Advertising Executive

"This is so much more than a book about networking. The nuggets contained in **Gargantuan Networking** are valuable, if not crucial, for a gargantuan life. Richard Possett has not just observed the principles on which he has written; he has learned them and lived them."

~ Robert White III, Oil and Gas Executive

"Richard is a wise and caring man aiming to support busy people in achieving success. This book is insightful and lighthearted. Packed with useful information and a wealth of knowledge. Individuals who can absorb and utilize the messages herein will no doubt lead more productive and rewarding lives."

~ Janet Ford, Real Estate Executive

"Networking is an art. Most of us, whether desiring to market our own businesses or as an employee for someone else, can use the advice contained in **Gargantuan Networking** as a springboard to achieving our life's goals. It is an easy read with precious gems of wisdom scattered throughout. Get it; read it; live it."

~ T. Reid Young, Cash Management Executive

"Mr. Possett demonstrates how networking is both a springboard and a safety net. It is really how business was always done. It is really how business will always be done."

~ James M. Hinds, Attorney

Gargantuan Networking

THE NETWORKING TRILOGY

Gargantuan Networking is part of the Networking Trilogy along with MORE LEADS ~ *The Complete Handbook for TIPS Groups, Leads Groups, and Networking Groups* and **Powerful People Are Powerful Networkers** ~ *Your Daily Guide to Becoming a Powerful Person*. To review one or all of these great books in the trilogy, please visit www.bepossettive.com or www.bepowerful.net. The trilogy speaks to the potential, the possible, and the practical in the networking process. The trilogy is all about the conceptual, concrete, and comprehensive of the networking process.

☙❧

Gargantuan Networking ~ The Teachings of *Karmic~the~Wise* As Recorded In *The Book of Lagniappe*. Translation by Richard Possett.

MORE LEADS ~ *The Complete Handbook for TIPS Groups, Leads Groups, and Networking Groups*. Written by Peter Biadasz.

Powerful People Are Powerful Networkers ~ *Your Daily Guide to Becoming a Powerful Person*. Co-authored by Peter Biadasz and Richard Possett.

Gargantuan Networking

The Teachings of

Karmic~the~Wise

As Recorded In

The Book of Lagniappe

Translation by Richard Possett

Foreword by Peter Biadasz

iUniverse, Inc.

New York Lincoln Shanghai

Gargantuan Networking
The Teachings of Karmic~the~Wise
As Recorded In The Book of Lagniappe

Copyright © 2006 by Richard W. Possett, Sr.

All rights reserved. No part of this book may be used or reproduced by any means, graphic, electronic, or mechanical, including photocopying, recording, taping or by any information storage retrieval system without the written permission of the publisher except in the case of brief quotations embodied in critical articles and reviews.

iUniverse books may be ordered through booksellers or by contacting:

iUniverse
2021 Pine Lake Road, Suite 100
Lincoln, NE 68512
www.iuniverse.com
1-800-Authors (1-800-288-4677)

ISBN-13: 978-0-595-38778-6 (pbk)
ISBN-13: 978-0-595-83159-3 (ebk)
ISBN-10: 0-595-38778-0 (pbk)
ISBN-10: 0-595-83159-1 (ebk)

Printed in the United States of America

DEDICATION

I am a very fortunate businessman. During my career in the corporate world, I had four very kind and talented mentors. These gentlemen were the prototypes of the modern entrepreneur and epitomized the criteria for achievement. They were men of inexhaustible work, knowledge, intellect, education, creativity, and personality. They "pushed the envelope" in business affairs, but obeyed the commercial rules and ethical standards of the day. They were risk takers and not hypocritical regarding their self-interest in gaining financial success. They saw themselves as men of integrity and purpose. They were willing to guide and coach the inexperienced during their business affairs so long as it didn't exacerbate their patience or impede their objectives. They taught me the importance of planning, knowing the cost of business, goal achievement, and good interpersonal communications. From them I learned a sense of optimistic realism versus the ethereal. I owe them a lot, and for that, I give thanks. It is to these gentlemen that I dedicate this book. I wish them all good health and happiness.

Richard Possett

FORE NOTE

Alagniappe (pronounced lan-yap) is a gift, a gratuity of sorts. **Gargantuan Networking** is meant to be just that for the reader. This is a book of tips on sound business and individual behavior. The writing is a blend of common-sensical wisdom in conjunction with sound networking procedures. Thus, **Gargantuan Networking** brings the reader some commercial best practices coupled with more than a few living life guideposts. The text focuses on ethical relationships and good conduct. And, networking is simply good human relations, both personal and professional. Hence, **Gargantuan Networking** is a book of gifts.

Karmic~the~Wise is a fictional business character. He was created in an effort to add some pizzazz to the text. His teachings are the learnings of the author. The book, **Gargantuan Networking**, therefore, is a gift to you from *Karmic~the~Wise*. Please read and enjoy! Now, a simple sidebar, for those of you that may be wondering; "KTW" is the initials of *Karmic~the~Wise*.

Richard Possett

Why Read This Great Book

Everything is for sale, everyone is negotiating, and everybody networks. And, if you are not networking, then you are most likely not fully working. We network to create lasting personal friendships and profitable professional relationships. We network on and off the job; on the golf course; at sporting and entertaining events; in meetings; and at business breakfasts, lunches, and dinners. We network at church, school, service clubs, industry associations, chamber of commerce meetings, TIPs groups, and seminars. It's ubiquitous! It is done everywhere by everybody. So, the challenge is to network more effectively and efficiently to achieve greater business success with a deeper and more fulfilling personal life style.

Currently, there are some really great networking publications in the marketplace. Because networking is a self-taught discipline, it would be helpful to your networking success to acquire and read these writings. Please see the suggested readings in the back of this book or merely go to the internet and "Google" the subject for specific insights.

The purpose of **Gargantuan Networking** is to "fill in the blanks" and "fill out the pages" of all the above aforementioned writings. **Gargantuan Networking** is not a substitute for these or any other networking literary works but, hopefully, a good supplement. Our goal is to complement these authors and give networkers a body of work to help them become better at the art of networking.

Reading this book will enhance your networking skills. It is meant to be a compass heading you in the right direction. The actual journey is yours. **Gargantuan Networking** contains an abundance of practical networking material, some professional and business advice, and a few bits of rumination on living life issues. You should find the subject matters enlightening, entertaining, and usable in your daily routines. Buy it, read it, apply it, have some fun, and make a lot of money with this book. Everybody networks in some mode or manner. Let's make the enterprise a profitable business and not just busy-ness for you. Let's make the endeavor fun for your living life. The helpful advice, tips, and anecdotes in this book will go a long way in achieving that objective. Read, enjoy, and be prosperous and happy at networking.

Richard Possett

FOREWORD

From the time we are born until the time we die, we all network in some form or fashion. Most network in a haphazard manner. That is, unorganized and unproductive. You have in your hands information that will help you educate yourself on how to be a more organized and productive networker. But, this is only part of the story.

You see, **Gargantuan Networking** is one-third of a trilogy written so that you can become the best networker you are **capable** of becoming. Notice that I didn't say you can become the best networker you think you can. In almost every instance in life, we have the capability of being better than we think. The question is then…"how can I become the best networker I am capable of becoming?"

If the Networking Trilogy was a sentence, then my book, **MORE LEADS**, would be an exclamation point, **Powerful People Are Powerful Networkers** would be a question mark, and **Gargantuan Networking** would be a period. **MORE LEADS** boldly instructs you with everything you need to know about starting and running a networking group. It also teaches you about the basics of how to be an organized and productive networker. **Powerful People Are Powerful Networkers** not only asks you many questions but also forces you to ask questions of yourself as you examine more deeply the details of being a proficient master networker. **Gargantuan Networking** fills in the networking self-educational gaps to ensure that you are well rounded and complete in the art of networking.

I met Richard Possett through networking. And even though we may be opposites in our approaches to networking due to differences in industries and personalities, the result of our networking is truly your gain. These books were written from our heads but inspired by our hearts. Enjoy the experience and become the best networker you are **capable** of becoming.

May you have the heart of a networker.

Peter Biadasz

Acknowledgements

A very special thank you goes to my wife Marilyn for all of her love and support.

Carol Collins, the word processing master. We have successfully worked together for nearly twenty years. She applies all the "elbow grease" and professional polish to my work.

Virginia Young, my good friend, who has devoted many-many hours and enthusiasm to editing and proofreading my literary work.

Cindy Reed, my long-term graphic artist, who has been extremely patient with my…"*I need it now*"…work schedules and projects.

I would like to recognize all my fellow networkers. Unbeknownst to them, I have listened carefully to all of their words and closely observed both their actions and deeds. In doing this, they have given me the networking insights to write this book.

To my partner in the Power Series, Peter Biadasz, I say congratulations. He was the tour-de-force in my writing about networking.

Richard Possett

CONTENTS

Part IV ~ The Cool Off

Part V ~ The Finis

Part I ~ The Proem

In the activity of networking, we develop personal friendships and create professional relationships. Thus, the personal and professional are entwined together and woven around one another for a connection of fun and profit.

~ KTW

Start to Finish

Starting is easy, but it's...
The last mile of the marathon,
The last yard to the end zone,
The last buoy in a regatta,
The last turn on the speedway,
The last inch to the cup,
The last foot to the dash,
The last second in the game,
The last pitch to the batter,
The last hill in the journey,
The last stand before the bell,
The last ledge to the summit,
...That counts; because if
You don't finish, it doesn't
Matter who is first or last.

~ KTW

PROLOGUE

Many-many years ago, in a land far, far away, there once lived a very wealthy Rajpoot by the name of *Karmic~the~Wise*. During his long and illustrious life, he flew-about on his magic carpet, peddling his goods and wares, from the Arabian Sea to the Bay of Bengal. Although the business was headquartered primarily in the New Delhi region, his geographical territory included India, Pakistan, Bangladesh, Kashmir, and Nepal. He was raised a pauper and became a renowned business Brahman. His family fame and fortune were built upon the holistic inter-relational philosophy of **Gargantuan Networking**. That is, the exchange of fun and profit from his personal (family and friends) and his professional (business acquaintances and associates) circles of influence or spheres of sway.

To *Karmic~the~Wise*, networking is meant to be a huge, helpful, and happy occasion. Its primary purpose is to develop symbiotic relationships producing synergistic rewards. The methodology is to create profitable business and personal contacts. To the king of connectivity, networking is the proactive marketing of you and what you do. It is all about communication and getting your name and that of your business known. It is the art of meeting people and benefiting from the information and links that you develop. These productive acquaintances are established to further the prime goal of the business enterprise, i.e., to enhance the bottom line.

Essential to **Gargantuan Networking** is the phenomenon known as the *cascading effect*. For *Karmic~the~Wise*, this notion was a highly effective commercial and personal doctrine. He felt that the *cascading effect* was, and would be for all time, a massive productive outcome brought about by the impact of a minute series of interconnected inputs, i.e., the sum of all the parts in the networking process. Then, all of these tiny tactics would waterfall into a major increase in outputs, e.g., great fame and fortune. To the discerning swami of sagacity, the *cascading effect* was something concrete vis-à-vis abstract. He knew that it generated real world benefits in the form of personal wealth, tangible and intangible.

For hundreds of years, the myriad of networking best practices, procedures, and policies used by *Karmic-the-Wise* were handed down by memory and word of mouth. Then, sometime in the middle of the 19th century, these business habits and customs were recorded by his disciples and published in *The Book of Lagniappe.*

This book contains comprehensive insights into **Gargantuan Networking** as profusely professed by *Karmic~the~Wise* and inspirationally inscribed in *The Book of Lagniappe.*

Richard Possett

INTRODUCTION

To network or not to network, that is the question. How much time, effort, and money do you invest into the endeavor? A lot, some, or none! No doubt, networking is time consuming and costs money. Will there be an adequate return on the investment? And, if so, how much ROI? These are all good questions. Now, let's look for some answers.

Networking isn't fast and easy. There is no quick buck in the process. You may accelerate the success curve through hyper participation, but it still takes elbow grease. In fact, networking is just marketing and, like marketing, it's relational with smart and hard work.

Networking is an association between persons built upon the shifting sands of understanding, comfort, and loyalty. This connection is maintained by the bedrock foundation of mutual respect, trust, and benefit. It isn't a rapid or swift development. It isn't free from trouble, anxiety, and pain. It's exacting, fickle and tedious. It's a personal choice.

Experience tells us that effective networking pays off handsomely. But, is it right for you? Does it meet your business needs and personal skills? For the process must be fully embraced to be successful. Like any other enterprise, a haphazard attempt will produce a slipshod result. Without a maximum undertaking, the end will be minimal. Here again, you decide.

The primary objective of this writing is to provide the reader with some important knowledge about the networking process. A secondary goal of the publication is to pass along a variety of pithy business pointers. A tertiary aim of the work is to furnish a few living life advisories. For networking is both personal and professional. These aggregate insights are meant to fully complement the networking activity. This is a book addressing specific networking matters, speaking to universal business material and commenting on life circumstances. It is a trifecta of interpersonal relations.

In the final analysis, it must be your general desideratum in life to produce the greatest possible value from any and all of your investments. This would be valid whether they are in time and money or personal and professional. This is very true about networking. The cost-benefit must make good dollars and sense.

After reading this book, you will be able to adjudicate if networking is the right activity for you. If it is, the material will give you solid information on how to be good, no great, at the networking process. If not, your savings from just reading **Gargantuan Networking** will be significant related to all the potential opportunity costs you would have incurred. If networking is good for you, may the experience be tremendously pleasant and tumultuously productive.

Richard Possett

Part II ~ The Warm Up

Your attitude towards networking, more than your aptitude, will define your relationship with fellow networkers. And, rest assured, your success in networking will be determined by the quality of those connections.

~ KTW

છ&

Memories

Each day begins, advances, and ends with moments cascading into memories. Make the best of them. In the day, as you climb the mountain, completely know your mission, competently under-stand your job and, then, carefully execute on that knowledge. For Leonardo da Vinci reminds us..."As a well-spent day brings happy sleep, so a life well used brings happy death." Make the best of it. Just for today, promise yourself to abide by the book, work smartly-hard, enjoy your friends, and have a lot of fun. Make the best of you in all you do! Please remember, moments make the memories and memories make the mortal.

~ KTW

CHAPTER ONE

Minute Morning Moments

Early, before sunrise, an owl perched on a limb. Seeing, for that rare few seconds, eyes-to-eyes before she flies off and is gone into the dusk of dawn.

At the first blush of morning, the birds of the woods twitter and trill in the trees, chirping the announcement to begin in their own special now and then song.

We see a still sole horse silhouetted against a red barn. The ground mist hangs close to a greenish brown pastureland. This sight interrupted by the city scent of smog.

The ear hears the tranquil sound of thick wind and close air moving intermittently among the branches and leaves. The breeze floats and flows dissipating the aurora fog.

Weaving water cascades and crashes with a thunderous cry as it dives and dies into the turf. Billions of billowing droplets create a prism of rainbow surf from the brighten sky.

Smells of breakfast waft gently and lightly along the road from who knows where as pangs of hunger ruminate on the mind. Alas, it is a sheer delight of flight in a cockcrow pace ply.

Sunlight reflected lunarscape adjacent to the lingering twinkle of the fleeting stars. The moon nods and the pulsars wink, all part of the wee small hours of celestial fun.

The hawk hovers, fence high, just above its break of day prey. Then it quickly drops and seizes the last grasps of life and flies off into the shadows of the forenoon sun.

A herd of horses goes galloping across the range, a strange ante meridiem sight at the city's edge. Their nostrils smoke and waving manes; this is a rare, raw and rural beauty on the run.

Prime time cracks through the dull mind as the body welcomes this extension of life. Yesterday is yore and tomorrow is tomorrow, but today has joyously begun.

Be super good, but get better.

~ KTW

Chapter Two

The Power of "WE"

In a group or team setting, "us" and "we" are more potent, powerful, and puissant than "I" or "me." "We" evokes a forceful synergy where the whole is greater than the sum of its parts. Joint action by a group of mobilized people will generate more productive results than that of sole individual effort. As people of commerce, we are obligated to harness this dynamism so as to produce the best of success.

Maximizing ownership wealth is the purpose and province of every businessperson. Therefore, the primary task and duty of everyone in the establishment is to optimize the franchise worth of the enterprise. To accomplish this mission, it takes commitment, competence, cooperation, creativity, communication, caring, courage, character, and, more importantly, connection.

CONNECTION is the natural interrelationship between the primal desires of the customer and the pecuniary interests of the owners, managers, associates, and suppliers of a commercial entity. Unfortunately, many of today's business people have become disconnected from their customers. These individuals fail to understand the basic association between their success and that of satisfying the needs and wants of their patrons.

Typically, professional men and women want prosperity and harmony, that is, wealth or ("w"). Given choices, they will choose justice and honesty, i.e., equity or ("e"). We believe that this is success, by definition, which is represented by ("s") and the product is "we." Therefore, s = we.

Generally, customers want to pay the lowest affordable price to purchase the highest obtainable quality of anything which is supported by the best available service. This is VALUE or ("V"), which is the full measure of PRICE, QUAL-ITY, and SERVICE or PQS. This is manifested in the formula, V = PQS.

To realize the objective of organizational franchise worth optimization, we all, that is, each and every person of commerce, must want and work for success. To be successful, we are required to deliver VALUE to the marketplace. Consequently, s = V.

Through the power of "we," an organization can become UNDISCON-NECTED with their customers. As shown above, we = s, PQS = V and V = s, and for this reason, V = we. Then, the exponent "n" is added to the power of "we." This expresses how many times "we" choose to meet the specific desires of our customers. Therefore, $V = (we)n$. As one can see, VALUE is the stone that encases PQS in a kernel germinating a unitary, dynamic, and three dimensional affirmative marketplace maelstrom leading to the best of success and "we" to the nth degree.

CHAPTER THREE

Your Job Description

"To Create Customers"

1. A *Customer* is the most important person in our business.

2. A *Customer* is not dependent on us, we are dependent on them.

3. A *Customer* is not an interruption of our work, they are the reason for it.

4. A *Customer* does us a favor when they call. We are not doing them a favor by serving them.

5. A *Customer* is part of our business, not an outsider.

6. A *Customer* is not a statistic, but a human being with feelings and emotions like our own.

7. A *Customer* is not someone to argue or match wits with.

8. A *Customer* is a person who brings us their wants. It is our job to fill those desires.

9. A *Customer* is deserving of the most courteous and attentive service we can give them.

10. A *Customer* is the life-blood of this and every other business.

11. A *Customer* is the paying patron, so fill their needs.

12. A *Customer* is not a problem, but an opportunity to succeed.

13. A *Customer* pays our bills, taxes, benefits, and payroll.

14. A *Customer* is a hidden treasure. Seek and enjoy the riches.

"Customers...they make all the difference!"

Tomorrow

Tomorrow just doesn't happen. It's the situation and station that we lay out. It's the vocational and familial infrastructure that we build. How we construct that base and those pathways of life has universal impact. It surely influences the builder, the traveler, and the journey's end. Please be certain to design, assemble, and handle with care, for life is fragile and will easily break.

~ KTW

CHAPTER FOUR

Networking Promises

I will accept the concept that there is no magic wand.

I realize tremendous networking results take time, effort, learning, and perseverance. To be a top networker, I must climb the mountain and not expect someone to wave a wand and magically transport me to the top.

I will trust good networking techniques.

I realize I may not use every networking technique effectively. I will continue to improve and practice proficient networking methods.

I will conscientiously read and listen to motivational material.

I know I must constantly discover new ideas and concepts about networking so I can better serve my network. I will listen to motivational tapes.

I will adhere to proven networking principles.

I will maintain the highest level of integrity. I will commit myself to finding ways of fulfilling my network's needs and requirements.

I will keep my networking approach natural.

I will remember that people make networking work.

I will see myself as a top networker.

I will be proud to be a networker regardless of this day's rejections or rebuttals.

I will celebrate every networking accomplishment.

I don't have to win big in networking to feel satisfaction. What matters is that it was a job well done. I will consider any advance in networking a victory.

I will pursue my dream to be a professional networker.

I will not allow networking defeats to slow my desire to become the best I can be. Any positives will negate all the negatives.

I will utilize all my networking tools.

I know a networking tool left idle does no work. I will use my personal skills, knowledge, and network of resources to enhance my networking abilities and associates.

CHAPTER FIVE

Networking Ground Rules

Leave the past behind.

> Old attitudes, positions, biases, mindsets, and beliefs should be destroyed and new ones created.

Display a winning attitude.

> In order to succeed in networking as a cohesive group, we all must have a positive state of mind.

Choose to grow through your life.

> Training is a never-ending story. It provides the growth tools and skills you need to profitably network.

Admit your mistakes.

> Be willing to accept responsibility without being defensive or contentious. Don't play the blame game.

Work together.

> Always be open to the ideas of others and understand that people's world-view, opinions, and limitations may differ.

Communicate effectively.

Essential to efficacious communication is candid talk and a true willingness to carefully listen as well as speak. This is the key to a successful networking group.

Be prepared for change as a permanent way of life.

To grow in living life is to change, which is scary. It requires a great personal risk. Choose to take it because there is nothing more certain in life than change.

Commit to value.

A commitment is a personal pledge, a promise. They appear in both our words and actions. Keep them!

Be trustworthy and show respect.

We are all part of the network. Stand behind the group and the individual members. Be loyal, involved, honest, and humble and make a big contribution.

Understand people perceive situations differently.

What you may be saying isn't as important as what people are hearing. In living life, it's not what she said. It's what he heard that makes all the difference. Therefore, say what you mean and mean what you say.

Chapter Six

Networking Crème de la Crème

Care more than others think wise.

Risk more than others assume safe.

Earn more than others consume.

Motivate more than others manage.

Energize more than others stigmatize.

Dream more than others believe practical.

Enlighten more than others teach.

Learn more than others want to know.

Act more than others acquiesce.

Compromise more than others combat.

Renovate more than others remodel.

Empathize more than others emphasize

Mint more than others mimic.

Expect more than others know possible.

Will Power

Think positive

AND

Be a positive doer.

When doing and in doubt, please remember

You can…You will…You're good.

IF

It is uncertain what you will
achieve in the enterprise

BUT

It is certain that if you don't try, you will not achieve it,
then just go ahead and do it!

Remember, there are no "**ands**"
"**ifs**" or "**buts**" in will power.

~ KTW

Chapter Seven

Networking Friends

Be friendly with the people with whom you associate, for if it weren't for them you may be a perfect stranger.

Strangers are just friends waiting to happen. Make them happen!

Make friends before you need them, for a friend is never known until one is needed.

A real friend is one who walks in when the rest of the world walks out.

A friend is someone who neither looks down, nor tries to keep up.

If all my friends were to jump off a bridge, I wouldn't jump with them. I'd be at the bottom to catch them.

The way to have friends is to be willing to lose some arguments, time, and things.

A friend is a person who can step on your toes without messing up your shine.

Everyone hears what they want to hear. Friends listen to what you say. Best friends listen to what you don't say.

You can acquire friendship with friendship, but never with silver and gold.

True friends are like diamonds and pearls, precious and rare. False friends are like the autumn leaves, expended and found everywhere.

A friend is someone who thinks you're a good egg, even though you're slightly cracked.

A friend is someone who knows the song in your heart and can sing it back to you when you have forgotten the words.

Friends are God's way of taking care of us. Be sure to take good care of your friends.

~ Pseudononymous

Essence

We may live in a life fantasy, not knowing the myths from the realities. Will time tell as the invention of history is left to the sages of the ages? What surprises hast truth, for there is nothing more mischievous than naked mysteries. It can alter perceptions, behavior, and the psyche. But this havoc is for naught because nothing changes tide and time. It may only help us to better understand the past as it relates to the present and it can be a beacon into the future.

~ KTW

Chapter Eight

Networking Just for Today

Just for today I will try to live this day in the present and not undertake all of life's past and future problems. I can resolve to do a lot of something positive for sixteen hours that will be productive and beneficial to living life in the here and now.

Just for today I will be happy. My state of mind is my sole responsibility and, therefore, I will make up my mind to be happy.

Just for today I will adjust myself to what is and not try to adjust everything to my own desires. I will take my life as it comes and fit myself to it.

Just for today I will try to strengthen my mind. I will study. I will learn something new and useful. I will not be a mental loafer. I will read something that requires effort, thought, and concentration.

Just for today I will exercise my soul in three ways: I will do somebody a good turn and not get found out; if anybody knows of it, it will not count. I will do at least two things I don't want to do—just for exercise. I will not show anyone that my feelings are hurt; they may be hurt, but today I will not show it.

Just for today I will be agreeable. I will look as well as I can, dress becomingly, talk low, act courteously, criticize not one bit, not find fault with anything, and not try to improve or regulate anybody except myself.

Just for today I will have a plan. I may not follow it exactly, but I will have it. I will save myself from hurry and indecision.

Just for today I will have a quiet half hour all by myself and relax. During this half hour I will try to get a better perspective of my life.

Just for today I will be unafraid. I will not be afraid to enjoy my lot and luck in life and to believe that as I give to the world, so the world will give to me.

~ Pseudononymous

Gift of Life

Yesterday is the past,
And lo, it went ever so fast.
Tomorrow is the future,
And behold, it can be ever so unsure.
But today is the gift of life,
That is why it is called the present.
Cherish it through accord and strife,
Knowing how and why it was sent.

~ KTW

Part III ~ The Plunge

Words and actions can be like oil and water; they don't mix. Actions speak louder than words. So, let your actions scream and have your words be silent.

~ KTW

The Basics

Doing the basics is the "WORK" in networking. For if you're not working on the basics, then you are not fully networking. By executing on the fundamentals, the work becomes the "FUN" of networking and the "FUNDS" from networking. Get it and give it! Never get bored with the basics. When we conquer the networking basics, the "razzle-dazzle" takes care of itself by itself. Remember, the only place networking comes before work is in the dictionary. Networking! Thank God for the swing of it; for the clamoring, hammering, and the ring of it; and for the beautiful sing of it.

~ KTW

✍✍

CHAPTER NINE

The Two Branes

Karmic~the~Wise felt there were two distinct schools of thought relative to networking. He termed one the *O'brane* and the other the *U'brane*. As a young businessman, the knight of nexus learned…that no matter how thick or thin you slice it, there are always two sides. Let's explain the two systems.

The *O'brane* worldview upholds the belief that all interpersonal human exchange is a networking opportunity. To them, the activity is omnipresent, thus the *O'brane*. It is a universalistic outlook towards networking. This is sort of a "shotgun" dragnet for business leads and referrals. As generalists, they believe that one networks in everything they do and everywhere they go. To the *O'branes,* it is a ubiquitous activity—a frequent, broad, and general pursuit. They liken it to mass marketing.

The *U'brane* philosophy espouses a narrower view of the networking universe. It is a selective system of principles for the conduct of networking. This view-point holds to a more specialized approach to generating business leads and referrals. As specialists, the *U'branes* are more pragmatic and practical. They are more utilitarian in their approach, stressing usefulness or utility over other considerations. They believe that networking is made for or aiming at utility, i.e., the *U'brane*. This school of thought compares their system to target marketing. That is, a more "rifle" approach to the activity.

Karmic~the~Wise understood that neither philosophy was right or wrong. The *O'brane* is at the far left of the spectrum and the *U'brane* is on the right. The king of connections understood there were a lot of "swirling grays" in the middle. Furthermore, he recognized that adhering to a certain belief is a relative choice and not an absolute option.

Like most things in life, it usually depends. The chosen system is influenced by the type of one's business. It is determined by available channels of distribution. It is contingent upon the law of probability. But, in the final analysis, the acid test is whether one approach is more efficient and cost-effective than the other method. The cost-benefit quotient should always rule.

What type of business do you conduct? It doesn't matter whether you are a service provider or product producer. What does matter is your market size and turnover. If you have an expansive market and a high turnover of trade, then the *O'brane* approach is more conducive to your success. Examples might be equipment sales, word processing, insurance, computer and internet services, and retailing mass merchandise. If your market is more selective with lower turnover rates, then pursue the *U'brane* system of networking. Illustrations of this type of business activity might be home lending, realty, security systems, financial planning, and title examination work.

When we look at the different networking venues or distribution channels, we need to be aware of the law of probabilities. That is, the ratio of the number of times a lead or referral will probably occur to the total number of possible occurrences in a specific gathering or network. If the probabilities are low, then we ignore the activity. Of course, if the chances are high, then we cultivate the event. The real question we need to ask ourselves is…"where do our customers hang out?" The answer for an *O'brane* would not be so important because they are interested in mass marketing. The response for an *U'brane* would be critical because they have a much more focused market to nurture. You go to where the highest numbers of customers are at any given time.

The bottom line for any enterprise is profit. Therefore, what is the highest and best use of your time and resources? This should dictate your business activities as an *O'brane* or *U'brane*. What channels of distribution and networking venues are the most economical? It is the time-tested cost-benefit formula. Your networking should produce a measurable increase in your business income. And, those revenues must exceed your business cost and expense associated with the networking activity. If you don't make a profit from networking, shame on you. If you don't know your cost of doing business, double shame on you. If you don't know the amount of revenue generated from the business activity, triple shame on you.

Whether you are an *O'brane* or *U'brane*, just use your brain to make the right choices for networking. Work hard, have some fun and make a profit. As

Karmic~the~Wise once said…"If you don't know where you are going, you will probably end up where you don't what to go." Therefore, be a smart networker regardless of whether you are an *O'brane* or *U'brane.*

"The Spectrum"

Where do you stand?

It's not the black and white that is problematic in networking, but all the swirling grays. They will determine your breadth of commitment to the people in the network.

~ KTW

CHAPTER TEN

The 'Mees' and 'Wees'

The Kalif of Jammu once referred to *Karmic~the~Wise* as one of the most sagacious business thinkers of the ages. He was talking about the wise one's ability to create the meaningful state of "we" from the mere status of "me." Fully understood, the successful progression of networking is culminated with the development of a "we" reality, for true networking takes place when there is a clear focus on the other person. This focal point creates a situation where the joint sum is greater than the individual parts. This condition produces functional networking. And, this occurs when one plus one equals three. Therefore, in the final analysis, networking propitiously manifests itself into a synergistic-symbiosis at which point the '*mees*' are transformed into the '*wees*.'

The metamorphosis of the '*mees*' into the '*wees*' is a metaphysical transformation of a relationship. This affinity can be for individual purposes, commercial trade, or both. It has its roots, not in a simple physical handshake, but in a proactive interpersonal promotion of one another's self and business. It is the conscientious development of interdependence between people unmistakably generating more personal and professional enterprise. This course of action is not static, but dynamic. The networking relationship is an ongoing process. It is an operation that *Karmic~the~Wise* divided into five phases. He called it the Five "C's" of Networking, which included the following steps:

1. Connection
2. Consultation
3. Commentary
4. Construction
5. Commitment

The first act in the process is the connection or association of persons. This is the intersection of people and the bond that binds. It is a relationship linking together common interests and goals. This nexus can formally take place in a TIPS group, business convention, trade show, networking function, fellowship meeting, industry association, and/or community organization. Informally, it may manifest itself anywhere that you may choose to network. It can happen unexpectedly and may take place frequently. Thus, to simply begin the process, one needs to step forward, go into the world, and meet people. As *Karmic~the~Wise* once said…"to go alone is to be alone in a world not alone."

The next phase in the operation is consultation. The objective in this stage is to gather information about potential new networkers. Here we meet and talk about mutual needs. We discuss bilateral benefits. We ask questions. We observe. We gather as much data as possible. Finally, we make a judgment as to the propriety of the person as a fellow networker. If so, we nurture the relationship. If not, we move on to the next.

When we define the word commentary, we mean a judgment made from a series of observations, analyses, and critiques. All this may sound somewhat too scientific, but it is the type of methodology that is needed to determine a solid networking relationship. Is the networking candidate a giver or taker? Does he or she have references? Is their vocation a fit for mutual benefit? What about the personal chemistry? Does the prospect have a track record of success? Does this candidate "get-it" as to networking? That is, do they fully understand the give and take that is necessary to make networking successful? Are they ready, willing, and able to make the appropriate investment of time and resources?

If the networking relationship is not based upon shared respect, interest, and benefit, then it is transitory and will collapse the moment the leads disappear. And, take it from experience, this type of prospect only wants unilateral referrals. Seldom do they give them. Check them out. It will save a lot of time in the long run. The process entails observing, evaluating, and choosing whether to continue the relationship or abort it.

Phase four is termed the construction stage. It is the manner and method in which the networking relationship is built. To start, we have a business breakfast, lunch, dinner, coffee, or drinks with our new fellow networker. We ask a lot of questions and listen carefully to all the answers. *Karmic~the~Wise* recommended that you make your own list, but here he offered a few sample questions you may consider asking.

✓ Where does he live?

✓ What does she do for fun?

✓ Does she have any pets?

✓ Does he like music, sports, or the theater?

✓ If so, what kind of events?

✓ What is her favorite kind of food?

✓ What movies does she like?

✓ Does he enjoy traveling?

✓ What type of books does she read?

✓ Where did he grow up?

✓ Where did he go to school?

✓ What was her childhood like?

✓ Why did she choose her profession?

✓ Does he have a family, brothers, or sisters?

✓ Did she go to college?

✓ If so, when and where?

The king of connections told us that we must take a genuine personal interest in the person. This is the first good step in developing a strong relationship. Next, we visit the new networker's place of business. We take a tour of the facilities, meet the boss, talk to coworkers, and just get to know our fellow networker much better. If need be, we tutor and mentor our colleague. We consider co-op advertising. We provide guidance on what networking venues to visit. For a short period of time, we chaperone our fellow networker to business events. We give leads and referrals. Doing all of these activities are the ways a long-term networking relationship is constructed. It is how we transform the 'mees' into the 'wees.'

The final phase in the process is commitment. This is a pledge or promise to do something. It is an obligation to a long-term involvement in the process of networking. A commitment is a responsibility, a duty, to a relationship. Specifically, we are talking about the relationship of networking.

A network is as strong as its weakest members. If some members are committed and others are not, the networking relationship can sustain such an imbalance for only a short period of time before the group breaks up. If one is reticent, reluctant, or resistant to the process, it will fail. The strength is total commitment to the network. You commit to help solve problems. You commit to create opportunities. You commit to be patient. You commit to participate. You commit to give and receive more leads. You commit to change the basic nature of your personal and professional relationships from the '*mees*' into the '*wees*' of networking.

If we want to take networking into a higher realm…beyond just meeting and greeting people…into the stratosphere where there is an exchange of energy and enterprise…then we must truly connect and commit to the activity. According to the time-tested Five "C's" of Networking prescribed by *Karmic~the~Wise*, the transmutation from the '*mees*' to the '*wees*' is not only possible, but highly predictable if the networkers work on it and make it work!

The Wiser Wager

The probable outcome of doing nothing is nothing. Conversely, the admissible result of doing something is something. The former has all the possibilities of failure. The latter has all the possibilities of success. Consequently, it is always preferable to do something vis-à-vis nothing in the course of life. It is the wiser wager.

~ KTW

"The Well"

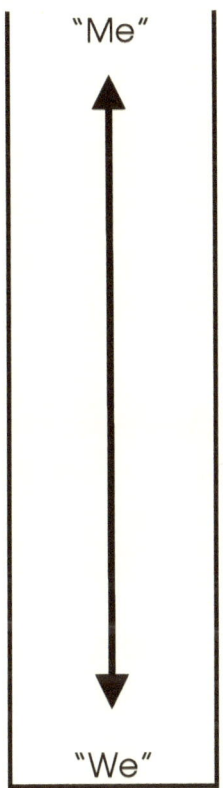

"Me"

"We"

How Deep Is Your Commitment?

How deep you dig the well from the surface of "me" to the bottom of "we" will define your true depth of loyalty and engagement in networking.

~ KTW

Perception

Our sole job is to create customers by fulfilling their value need.

In the mind of the customer, perception is indeed reality.

So, from a business point-of-view, perception is everything.

The challenge, then, becomes to create the perception that shapes the reality meeting the value need.

~ KTW

CHAPTER ELEVEN

Join-In

Karmic~the~Wise told us to join in and don't just attend. Simply going to meetings and being a "bump-on-a-log" or joining the "comfort-crowd" is counterproductive. This type of person might as well stay in the office or, better yet, get a new job. The majestic marvel of networking challenges us to dare to share and partake in the game of networking each day. He said it is critical to meet and greet as many people as practical in each networking venue. One should network everywhere according to their *O'brane* or *U'brane* proclivities. Please don't sit on the bench or stand on the sidelines, he explains.

The noble knight of nexus wanted us to get into the game of networking in commanding ways. Make a splash, shape a headline, and have some major impact in our lives. It was his steadfast belief that all of us should be "wave-makers" and not simply "wave-riders." He felt that to be passive in networking, as in life, was to be a thief. For a do-nothing networker steals time and money from his associates. And, this type of person should be exiled to the Land of Nothingness. They give nothing and, therefore, should get nothing less.

Karmic~the~Wise chided us to create the nexus tsunami. It is our right to smash into events and break a leg. It is our responsibility to stub our toe, cause the concussion, and bloody our nose. In that light, the imperial wizard of networking admonished us to step forward, take charge, lead by example, roll up the sleeves, pitch in, help out, follow through, give it your all, stay the course, accept the onus, start to finish, and, most essentially, give to get. In this, we will create a flourishing *cascading effect* on wealth building in our lives and those of our networking associates.

To-Do

I am only one, but I am one;

I cannot do everything

But I can do something.

What I can do, I ought to do

And what I ought to do

I will do to the best of my ability.

~ KTW

CHAPTER TWELVE

Speak-Up

Speak-up about you and what you do. Keep it simple and straightforward, the "KISS" approach. Broadcast your personal résumé and business commercial loud and clear. For if you don't smartly self-promote, nobody else will do it for you. Don't be afraid to toot your horn and tout your business.

One of the greatest human fears is rejection. It is pervasive in life. *Karmic~the~Wise* was right-on when he postulated…"Be unafraid of fear, for fear is nothing but fear itself." He further proclaimed that non-acceptance is not about us, the rejectee. But, it is all about the other person, the rejector. It's the rejector's choice. You as the rejectee, graciously, with peace of mind, accept the decision. It is your choice to choose.

Taking this good advice to heart, the august potentate of networking reminds us to be always fearless. For fear is only a state of mind of self-inflicted pain. Don't be a masochist and don't practice sadism. Furthermore, on all occasions be certain to rebuff rejection. It is not about you. Simply move on to the next situation.

Karmic~the~Wise told us in no way to be frightened of getting to know people. Never be afraid to let people know who you are and your vocation and avocation. Always ask for the business. Through this, you will surely grow and prosper in all facets of your life.

Pushing the Envelope

The phrase "pushing the envelope," which comes from aviation, refers to pushing an aircraft beyond the "envelope" of design limits. Nowadays, the phrase is shorthand to some people for pushing against, what they believe are, sound personal and commercial practices, ethical conventions, and public standards of taste. Therefore, it is critical that we architect our commercial and cultural boundaries with intellect, virtue, and grace.

~ KTW

Chapter Thirteen

Stand-Out

How do you differentiate yourself? What is the unique selling proposition for your company? What sets you apart from the crowd? How do you brand you and what you do? Do you have any WOWpower, that dynamism, compulsion and capability to make things happen and to get things done?

Karmic~the~Wise asked…do you have a unique selling proposition ("USP"), some remarkable trade appeal, a special marketing offer ("SMO"), or a distinctive business value that can arouse interested enthusiasm in people to buy your product and/or service? If so, this is your COWABUNGA. Show and tell this feature in all you do. It will help create the attention, interest, desire, and action necessary to make the sale straightaway.

Now, what about a prominent portion of MOJO? This is that certain personal attribute that gives you some particular charm and positive character that people enjoy, trust, and respect. It is the magical power that, along with the COW-ABUNGA, propels your private success over and above mediocrity.

For most of us, these two characteristics of WOWpower are not simply givens. They must be assiduously cultivated and developed. The outstanding overlord of networking mildly reproves us to work on these personal qualities and business methods every day because it's the business of getting business. As in life, it's much to-do about them.

All the positive karma that takes place within and about the COWABUNGA and MOJO will seal any deal. For it's your WOWpower that helps make the money. And, closing the sale is the key goal in any economic enterprise. If you don't believe *Karmic~the~Wise*, just ask the BOSS!

Always

Always is every moment,
    until the end of time.
Always is always only,
    that we will be fine.
Always is universal,
    but very specific to me.
Always is an affinity of networking,
    which is the reality of we.

~ KTW

CHAPTER FOURTEEN

Focus-On

Focus on the human element. Conscientiously and with much intensity, zero-in on people, personalities, and profiles. Unless one has a photographic mind, these three small steps take a lot of arduous effort, time, and skill. Upon meeting someone, can you quickly and clearly recall their name at the very next encounter? Most people can't! What about their business? Do they provide a service or produce a product? What is the name of their company? If you are unfamiliar with the people you meet, then you cannot build your business. And, helping people expand the enterprise is what networking is all about.

The primary purpose of networking is to develop symbiotic relationships that produce synergistic rewards. Symbiosis is the intimate toiling together in close association with different businesses for mutual economic advantage. Networking synergism is when the cooperative action or force is greater than the sum of the parts. It is the one plus one equals three of you and me networking together profitably. Symbiotic-synergy is manifested in the acronym *IRU~RME*. This is expressed as follows.

I	~	Introduction	Meeting & greeting a contact
R	~	Recognition	Identifying that particular person
U	~	Understanding	Knowing their business well
R	~	Referring	Providing productive referrals
M	~	Motivation	Inciting ongoing mutual success
E	~	Equity	Giving & receiving valued leads

People crave to be recognized, rewarded, and remembered. *Karmic~the~Wise* told us to zealously learn to relate a name to a face and then, that individual to their business. Finally, the great one of networking commands that we be certain to refer, refer, and refer again. This is the reward. Always remember to help and support your fellow networker. Actively aid them in the achievement of their personal goals and business objectives.

Succeeding with symbiotic-synergy is a continuous conscious connection with the business community. There are four stages in the method.

Stage 1   Contacting and meeting people
Stage 2   Connecting a name to a face
Stage 3   Cognizance of their business
Stage 4   Conscientiously providing referrals

Karmic~the~Wise pronounced that networking is a process that takes preparation, perspiration, practice, persistence, patience, and perseverance to be profitable. It was his true belief that the professional networker continuously follows the four stages in the circle of networking.

A wise man knows everything, but a shrewd one everybody.

~KTW

CHAPTER FIFTEEN

Query and Probe

Greet people, ask questions, and then listen and learn. *Karmic~the~Wise* cued us to be valiant, vigilant, and venerable. When you walk into a gathering, survey the venue, pick that unknown solitary individual, approach them and introduce yourself. Stay out of the cozy-zone. Don't gravitate into the comfortable crowd.

When the introductions are complete, ask questions! Query this new contact with all of the what, where, when, who, how, and why conversation catechisms. Then, listen and learn.

This method would be something like the following:

> HELLO, my name is *Karmic~the~Wise*. What is your business? Where are you located? When did the entity start up? Who established the company? How long have you been with the firm? Why did you pick this type of occupation?

Sooner, rather than later, this structured conversation begins to flow naturally and takes on a life of its own. When this happens, you have created a new source of business, a loyal associate and, most likely, a very good friend.

The sagacious one said…"Don't forget to ask the contacts for a business card. And, by gosh-sakes, supply them with one of yours." Whenever you happen to return to the office, be certain to quickly follow up with the contacts by telephone or correspondence. Then, place them in your database and stay in close contact with your contacts.

One and one equals three when it's you and me in the radical relational reality of "we."

~ KTW

Chapter Sixteen

Inculcate the Basics

Jump into your car and head out to the nearest public library. On your way, stop off at the neighborhood office supply store and pick up a packet of 3 x 5 index cards. It's assumed that you have a pen in hand. When you get to the library, pull down the Webster's New World Dictionary. Sit at a table and make yourself comfortable.

Let's regress and get some background on our assignment. At the core of **Gargantuan Networking** is the *Proposition of the "9-Ps."* The *"9-Ps"* are the very basics. They form the fundamental foundation of the networking process.

We all know that a proposition is a plan of action or proposal to do something (input) in return for some gain (output). In the networking process, knowledge is the input and its application is the output. It is both cause and effect. That is, you know; therefore, you succeed. The concept is fairly simple. It's the work of inculcating the basics that is difficult. We need to understand to be productive. Properly applied, knowledge is power.

Here is the assignment. At the top of nine index cards, write the following terms:

- ✓ Participation
- ✓ Perception
- ✓ Pro-action
- ✓ Promotion
- ✓ Pondering
- ✓ Partiality
- ✓ Peculiarity
- ✓ Process
- ✓ Purpose

Now, carefully look up and study each word in the dictionary. Then, write the definition of the term on the appointed 3 x 5 index card. Over the next few weeks and months, inculcate each word into your brain. Think how each term specifically relates to networking. Slowly and surely, you will come to internalize the proposition into everyday networking practices. Give it a try; it really works! Get it and give it!

Here are the expressed meanings of the terms as they relate to **Gargantuan Networking.**

Participation ~ to share with others in the business activity of networking for mutual benefit.

Perception ~ to become aware of the value of networking through observation.

Pro-action ~ taking the initiative to be a wave-maker and not a wave-rider.

Promotion ~ to help bring about growth and prosperity in the practice of networking.

Pondering ~ to consider carefully whether networking is a profitable undertaking.

Partiality ~ the obligation to favor networking group members with business referrals.

Peculiarity ~ this is the quality of being distinctive when networking.

Process ~ the particular method of doing networking for fun and profit.

Purpose ~ engaging in the process of networking with resolution and determination.

CHAPTER SEVENTEEN

Goal to Gold

The advice from *Karmic~the~Wise* was for us to see the vision and know the mission. Then, he advised us to understand the actual ambition we have for engaging in the practice of **Gargantuan Networking**.

What are we trying to accomplish? How do we intend to achieve our objective? Do we have an understanding of the necessary? Are we ready, willing, and able to handle the task at hand? The wise one asked us to step back, survey the situation, and develop the purpose as it relates to you and what you do. This, of course, assumes that networking is the right fit in the marketing mix. Now, go into detail on an action plan with time bound strategies and tactics. Plan your work and work your plan!

With a blueprint in hand, it is time to mine the goal. We must start digging real hard and heavy to tap into the mother load. It is a formidable task to excavate the precious materials from networking. Here are some suggestions, a *Karmic~the~Wise* how-to-do list to uncover the many business and personal riches.

- ✓ Attend Meetings
- ✓ Do Round-Robins
- ✓ On-Site Visits
- ✓ Congregate
- ✓ Provide Leadership
- ✓ Enlist & Enroll
- ✓ Work-Work-Work
- ✓ Pass Business Cards

- ✓ Exchange Information
- ✓ Co-op Advertising
- ✓ Dutch Connections
- ✓ Communicate
- ✓ Volunteer
- ✓ Preach & Teach
- ✓ Refer-Refer-Refer
- ✓ Sow-to-Reap

The exalted one of networking said an enthusiastic networker doesn't labor in the "caverns of coal" to merely make their daily bread. But, they craft their trade in the "goal mines" to create wealth. True networkers mine the GOAL to get the Gold! Please keep in mind that our goal is to develop symbiotic relationships that produce synergistic rewards.

Venture Vision

Ingenuity should always usher in the enterprise. But first, we must truly be inspired and believe in the task at hand. To conquer the concept, we cannot only stare at the stars—we must step up the stairs to them. Secondly, a metamorphosis should transpire, moving the endeavor from the abstract to the concrete. The vision needs to be hunted by the venture. Finally, energy comes after imagination in the tour de force with more perspiration than inspiration. We must perspire to retire, so shoot for the moon and even though you might fall short, you may just become a shining star. It happens because you not only see it, but you do it!

~ KTW

CHAPTER EIGHTEEN

Get = Give

Gargantuan Networking is all about helping people. It is a selfish concern for the welfare of others. For networking does have an element of self-interest. We plug others to pitch ourselves. It is what *Karmic~the~Wise* called the *alter-all*.

In the *alter-all*, we really make different our business practices to enhance the outcomes. That is, we change the focus of our work habits away from ourselves. We focus on others. In the realm of reality, it is the state of "we" vis-à-vis the status of "me." By transferring our energies from me, we first give and then receive. But, this is undertaken for mutual advantage. We help people to help us. It is done for the benefit of both you and me.

In the *alter-all*, "you and me" are parts of a whole that are tenaciously entwined. They are conjoined and, therefore, inseparable. To pull them apart into individual units would mutate the *alter-all*. Then we no longer have symbiotic-synergy, but transmutation into egotism, where the self only matters. And, to *Karmic~the~Wise*, this was self-defeating behavior.

The supreme pontiff of networking said we should start out each day with the question…"who am I going to help today?" Then, at day's end, we need to answer the following…"who did I help this day?" For in the *alter-all*, generosity begets reciprocity. It is a time-tested cause and effect phenomenon. A great many years ago, *Karmic~the~Wise* proclaimed the Golden Rule of **Gargantuan Networking** to simply be…GET *equals* GIVE.

Success

Success is speaking words of praise,
    And cheering other people's ways.
Success is doing the best you can,
    With every project and task at hand.
Success is silence when speech can hurt,
    And politeness when someone is curt.
Success is deafness when scandal flows,
    Having sympathy with others' woes.
Success is courage when disaster falls,
    Knowing the fits of nature's laws.
Success is patience when the hours are long,
    Making the best with laughter and song.
Success is found in the time of prayer,
    And also in happiness and despair.
Success in all of life is achieved,
    By what we gave and not received.

~ KTW

CHAPTER NINETEEN

Reciprocity

"When You're Good to Mama"

Ask any of the chickies in my pen
They'll tell you I'm the biggest mother hen
I love 'em all and all of them love me
Because the system works
The system called reciprocity...

Got a little motto
Always sees me through
When you're good to Mama
Mama's good to you.

There's a lot of favors
I'm prepared to do
You do one for Mama
She'll do one for you.

They say that life is tit for tat
And that's the way I live
So, I deserve a lot of tat
For what I've got to give

Don't you know that this
Hand washes that one too
When you're good to Mama
Mama's good to you!

If you want my gravy
Pepper my ragout
Spice it up for Mama
She'll get hot for you

When they pass that basket
Folks contribute to
You put in for Mama
She'll put out for you

The folks atop the ladder
Are the ones the world adores
So boost me up my ladder, Kid
And I'll boost you up yours

Let's all stroke together
Like the Princeton crew
When you're strokin' Mama
Mama's strokin' you

So what's the one conclusion
I can bring this number to?
When you're good to Mama
Mama's good to you!

Lyrics from the musical "Chicago."

CHAPTER TWENTY

The Raison D'être

Karmic~the~Wise reminded us of the all-important cosmic concerns. First, what's the reason for **Gargantuan Networking**? Why do we do it? And, second, what is the methodology? How is it done? Finally, what justifies participation, i.e., the cost-benefit?

It is the firm belief of the great sage of networking that one engages in the process to make MONEY, although it is a healthy practice to have fun while one is fully employed in the work of networking.

Next, we need to pick the right venue because networking gatherings can range from good to bad. Here are the major types of networking groups:

1. Service Fellowships
2. Community Organizations
3. NPOs
4. TIPs Groups
5. Industry Associations

Service fellowships, like Rotary and Kiwanis, are generally, at best, mediocre gatherings to seek out new business. These groups are populated by retired people who are more interested in community service than economic enterprise for our business.

Community entities, like the Chamber of Commerce, can be wonderful networking opportunities. In their meetings, they have a large and diverse group of businesspeople. These individuals and firms have like-minded goals, that is, to grow and prosper in their companies. The Better Business Bureau is a good example of a networking platform that is not suited to promoting your business. The firm is an arbiter of disputes between consumers and companies. It is not a conduit of connections and referrals.

Non-profit organizations or NPOs are only "so-so" when it comes to networking effectiveness. Affiliations, such as Junior Achievement and Big Brothers and Sisters are, rightfully so, focused on their not-for-profit mission and not creating wealth for their benefactors. Be wary or understand the payoff when allocating time and money for networking to these types of organizations.

A TIPs group is a more informal cluster of persons that is dedicated to the exchange of business referrals. If it is done effectively, this type of networking can be profitable. Otherwise, involvement in the TIPs process can be frustrating and incapable of producing adequate results.

There are two types of industry associations. One is cooperative and the other is competitive. Cooperative entities can beneficially help and support the business bottom line. They would feed economic activity to the enterprise. This would be like a realtor referring business to a mortgage banker. A competitive association would be a group of similar companies joining together for political, social, or industry purposes. These are birds of a feather that are flocking together. They all want the same worm. Not much cooperative business is generated in this type of gathering. It should be a low priority.

To "B2B" or "B2C" is another question. Your target market can have a great impact on the type of networking you do in your business life. The customer audience can also influence the kind of networking group you might join. Please remember, the purpose of networking is to generate quality leads and business referrals. From these leads and referrals, we create sales and bottom-line results for ourselves and the enterprise. Networking should be money in your wallet for business, home, and pleasure.

"B2B" commerce is between two businesses, i.e., vendor and client. Commercial telecommunications equipment would be sold by a merchant, middleman, or manufacturer to an end user. These entities are generally two commercial businesses. This could also be true of computer hardware and software, office machines (facsimiles and copiers), office supplies, accounting and payroll systems, and many, many more types of goods and services.

"B2C" trade is an exchange of economic activity between individual consumers and businesses. Retail and mortgage banking are two good examples. Clothing, grocery, shoe, and drug stores are some further illustrations of "B2C" trade. When a business sells and a person buys, you generally have a "B2C" transaction.

So what is your particular target? Does your networking venue meet the needs of your market? You could be a "B2Ber" and be in a networking group that is really focused on consumers. On the other hand, you could be a "B2Cer" and most of the people in the network are interested in commercial, and not consumer business. It is important to take stock of your networking investments and make certain they meet your specific needs.

The truth of the matter is that most networking groups and venues are composed of both "B2B" and "B2C" types of people. What is important is that you think about the composition and make the right judgment about participation. Your efforts and resources must be maximized. Networking is an investment of time and money. Let's be certain that we get the highest ROI from the activity.

In sports, some experts would say that a good defense is the best offense. Philosophically speaking, this may work well in athletics and games. But, quite frankly, in the real world of business it may all depend. There are times when we need a superior offense and a time when we need a stellar defense. In fact, there can be particular situations when we need them both.

When we start a business, it is essential that we have an outstanding offense to garner market share. While commerce is starting up and growing, we should begin to start thinking about protecting the hard-earned business. Once we hit critical mass, then we need to send in the defense to guard our economic gains.

The type of networking we do may be a function of where we are on the business development curve. In the beginning, we may need a networking venue that is long on growth and short on protection. The Chamber of Commerce and a high-powered TIPs group may be the ticket to success.

When we reach the point where the minimum amount of effort produces maximum monetary success, then we may need a defensive marketing strategy. Here is where PR, community organizations and service fellowships can be helpful. As always, we pick our own poison. Happy networking!

In the final analysis, we must examine the financial and relational return on the time, money, and effort contributed to the networking endeavor. In other words, what benefits accrue from the investment? The answer can be some, none, or a lot. If there is little or no ROI, then you must reconsider the networking practice or the venue as a viable use of valuable resources.

Persistent networking pays, but it takes perseverance.

~ KTW

CHAPTER TWENTY-ONE

Net-WORK-ing Works

As you cast your nets far and wide to snare business leads, ask yourself…"what is the key result area in the networking process?" For *Karmic~the~Wise*, the pivotal unit in the word, networking, was "WORK!" Clearly, it's the excruciating physical and mental effort exerted, along with the time and money expended, that is necessary to make **Gargantuan Networking** a purposeful and profitable enterprise. But, the payoff can be worth the work!

The work in networking can be outlandishly rewarding in astonishing ways. You can be blindsided with the benefits. **Gargantuan Networking** can put you in the right place at the right time for serendipitous rewards.

Karmic~the~Wise professed the lesson to never underestimate the unexpected consequences of a well-intended action. This is especially true when the outcome is most favorable. Such a propitious event is termed a *marvelous miracle* in **Gargantuan Networking**. It is the result of much effort. For the harder and smarter one works, the luckier one gets. To illustrate, let's review a few real life examples of this type of happening, the *marvelous miracle*.

Jack & Jill

Jack and Jill went up and down a number of hills together. During those episodes, they never did any business with one another. Jill was an exceptionally successful real estate agent. Mortgage banking was Jack's occupation. Over the years, these two professionals ran into each other at many different business gatherings. Jill was always happy with her financing arrangements. Then, they unexpectedly met and talked at a networking function they independently attended and it happened. Jill had changed her business environment and was struggling with a new selling paradigm. She discussed it with Jack, and he provided a viable solution to her dilemma. Now Jack and Jill are doing business together.

Stan & Oliver

As a financial consultant, Donavan was invited to speak on a very prestigious national government housing panel in Washington, D.C. If he attended, his business would have to pay the travel expenses for a three-day coast-to-coast trip. He declined the invitation. It was too expensive. Subsequently, he was convinced by his business associates to reconsider. Donavan went and spoke to the group. At the end of the session, he was approached by Stan and Oliver. They asked his advice on a major problem they were experiencing in their organization. He gave it, they liked it, and Donavan's firm was awarded a very large consulting contract.

When Harry Met Sally

Sally walked into the general meeting of the professional association she recently joined. Because she was new, Sally recognized very few people. Using a tip from **Gargantuan Networking**, she surveyed the room and saw a solitary person standing by himself. She wandered over and introduced herself to Harry. She went through the conversation catechisms. Sally queried, listened, and learned. Then, this general discussion turned to real specific business. Harry had an opportunity that Sally could exploit to their mutual benefit. A few days later, they met again to review the situation. Sally made a proposal that Harry accepted. This one happenstance paid for the entire cost of involvement for Sally in this professional association for years. It truly was a marvelous miracle of networking.

Dick and Jane

Jane was attending an early morning networking function, and she was introduced to Dick. This was his first time at the early-bird gathering. They chatted and then went their separate ways. Later in the day at another networking function, she recognized and approached Dick. They talked about Dick's business and his future plans. It seems that Dick was opening a number of coffee shops in the local market. In this type of situation, most people need working capital. This was true of Dick's business. As a capital venture executive, Jane was in a position to potentially provide assistance. They scheduled another meeting and struck a mutually beneficial deal. It was serendipitous networking at its best. This is another example of the *marvelous miracle* as taught by **Karmic~the~Wise.**

The moral of these four stories is that we never know when we will be blindsided with the benefits of networking. It is all part of the *marvelous miracle* in **Gargantuan Networking.** Partake, profit and enjoy!

The Business of Commerce at Work

It gives us adversity and opportunity, chance and choice, rights and responsibilities, failure and success, poverty and wealth, victory and defeat, and the spirit to dare, endure and rise above the ordinary.

~ KTW

Chapter Twenty-two

The Doom Prophecy

Developing a successful network is a process that requires time, talent, and treasure. If someone is not ready, willing, and/or able to make this type of commitment, chances are they will fail at the endeavor. On the other hand, if the people in an alliance have made the true leap from the static association of "you" and "me" into the dynamic reality of "we," in both energy and cognizance, the probability of making and molding a robust and long lasting networking infrastructure, that will pass the test of time, are very high. With a real understanding of the day-to-day necessities of networking and with true engagement, the networker can take the enterprise to an advanced level.

There are quite a few people who become quickly discouraged and disenchanted with networking. It's because they do not know how to properly network. In addition, they never make the effort to learn about the process. Networking is not taught in any school venue or on the job. Generally, it is a self-taught discipline.

Think of the networking process as a business enterprise. Here is what you do in business, day-in and day-out:

- You have a business plan. It contains a mission, values, goals, strategies, and tactics. Do the selfsame for networking.

- You enter into business agreements, promises, and pledges. Do the selfsame for the network.

- In business, you define roles and responsibilities. Everyone has a job description. Do the selfsame for networking.

- The business has structure, systems, operations, policies, and procedures. Who is the leader? Who sets policy and develops procedures? Do the selfsame for the network.

- Every business must generate revenues, know their cost of doing business and make a fair profit. Do the selfsame for networking.

- Each business has a system of internal controls, objectives, and tools to measure success. Do the selfsame for the network.

Carry over all of your best practices from the business into your networking activities. If you don't, I will make a foreboding prognostication: you are DOOMED to fail. This is because you didn't build a solid day-to-day foundation in your networking structure and relationships.

Nothing in networking happens without engagement.

~ KTW

CHAPTER TWENTY-THREE

Dead Reckoning

In the pre-technological times, air and sea travelers navigated by a technique known as "Dead Reckoning." Simply stated, a navigator lays out an intended course from point A to point B. Then they determine the heading that will take them to their destination. The navigator can calculate how long it will take to get to journey's end by using the expected speed and distance. Ideally, they can fly or float at the calculated predetermined heading and speed. When the predetermined time has expired, they should have reached their objective. Of course, fuel consumption must be considered.

In the real world, there are factors that can confuse the plan. In the air, we have cross/head/tailwinds to disrupt the course. On the water, there are both winds and currents that can cause problems. A good pilot would check with meteorology to anticipate climatic conditions and adjust the trip plan accordingly. It is advisable to ascertain landmarks (distance and location) to verify the trip plan. Each checkpoint along the route is an opportunity to refine the plan.

If a navigator is lax, or the weather is bad where they cannot see their landmarks, it is highly probable they will not reach their destination. Poor flying or sailing by not maintaining a steady speed or a constant heading can also influence arrival. Depending on the circumstances, the pilot could find himself or herself in real trouble, i.e., low fuel, rough terrain, adverse weather, and/or enemy territory. Therefore, all pilots, whether by water or air, know that "If I don't reckon right, I'm dead."

This maxim is also deadly true in networking. A networker that doesn't reckon right with their words and actions (commitment, loyalty, and participation) will die!

Essentially Essential

The first essential, of course, is to know what you want.
The second essential, of course, is to know how to do
   it.
The third essential, of course, is to do it.
The fourth essential, of course, is to do it right.
The fifth essential, of course, is to do it right now.

~ KTW

Chapter Twenty-four

Planning Statement

Here we are trying to look around the bend and see over the hill. What do we see for us in **Gargantuan Networking?** What's the gain? Where's the pain? With the proper preparation and productive practice, networking may be profitable. It will take WORK! Here is the plan.

VISION

To create an everlasting sphere of sway composed of a massive group of stakeholders dedicated to mutual growth and prosperity.

MISSION

The purpose is to develop symbiotic relationships producing synergistic rewards. The charge is to <u>effectively</u> utilize the networking paradigm in an <u>efficient</u> manner so as to generate exponential personal and financial results from the endeavor.

GOAL

Our objective is to identify serviceable networking venues, constituents, and mechanisms, and then utilize the teachings and lessons of *Karmic~the~Wise* in their employ.

STRATEGY

1. Be smartly selective
2. Make a strong commitment
3. Join-in and don't just attend
4. Speak-up about you and what you do
5. Stand-out from the crowd
6. Focus-on names, faces, and businesses
7. Query and probe
8. Fully inculcate the basics
9. Mine the GOAL to get the Gold
10. Live the GET = GIVE Rule
11. It's reciprocity, not generosity
12. Know the Raison d'être
13. Note net~WORK~ing works
14. Avoid Mr. Doom and Gloom
15. Don't dead reckon

TACTICS

1. Create Connections
2. Develop Relationships
3. Build Trust
4. Help Others First
5. Make More Money
6. Have Some Fun

Planning is like God, mother, and apple pie. Everybody is for it, but few do it. If you don't plan your work and work your plan, your work will work you instead of you working the work. It is your choice to choose because otherwise you will get worked-out of working.

Part IV ~ The Cool Off

Make yourself a better person and know who you are before you try to know someone else and expect them to know and trust you.

~ KTW

Raison D'être

The mission of the enterprise and the purpose of its people is to provide maximum value to their customers. Value is the full measure of price, quality, and service. By providing high quality services and products, at the best available price, supported by highly competent and responsive customer service, the enterprise will grow and prosper. Consequently, return on investment is maximized, which inures to the benefit of customers, associates, and shareholders. Value is gratuitous. It is not an endowment, but it is gratis. What is costly to the enterprise are all the actions that do not add value. Therefore, value is the only profitable ware of the enterprise.

~ KTW

Chapter Twenty-five

Networking Lessons Learned

- I've learned that you cannot make someone like you. All you can do is be someone who can be liked.

- I've learned that no matter how much I care, some people just don't care back.

- I've learned that it's not what you have in your life but who you have in your life.

- I've learned that you can do something in an instant that will give you life-long heartache or hope.

- I've learned that no matter how thick or thin you slice it, there are always two sides.

- I've learned that it's taking me a long time to become the person I want to be.

- I've learned that it's a lot easier to react than it is to think. Watch the reaction to the action.

- I've learned that you should leave loved ones with loving words. It may be the last time you see them.

- I've learned that you can keep going long after you think you can't.

- I've learned that we are responsible for what we do, no matter how we feel.

- I've learned that either you control your attitude or it controls you.

- I've learned that regardless of how hot and steamy a relationship is at first, the passion fades and there had better be something else.

- I've learned that it takes years to build up trust, and only seconds to destroy it.

- I've learned that you can get by on charm for about fifteen minutes. After that, you'd better know something.

- I've learned that you shouldn't compare yourself to the best others can do but to the best you can do.

- I've learned that it's not what happens to people that's important. It's what they do about it that really matters.

~ Pseudononymous

Chapter Twenty-six

Networking Thoughts of the Day

- The best things in life aren't necessarily things.

- Minds are like parachutes, they only function when open.

- We cannot direct the wind, but we can adjust our sails.

- He who laughs…lasts. Long laughs are long lasting.

- It takes both rain and sunshine to make a rainbow.

- Life offers us the opportunity to do work worth doing.

- Years wrinkle the skin. To give up interest wrinkles the soul.

- A gossip is a person with a keen sense of rumor.

- Make every moment count. We live by moments, not minutes.

- Live life to the edge of all possibility. It is possible.

- Rise above the obstacles in life and focus on the positive.

- Discover a new person, place, or thing…just discover.

- See it big and keep it simple and straightforward.

- Dare to be adventurous and adventure won't scare.

- We will not know unless we begin. So, let's get started.

- Set goals, challenge yourself and achieve them.

- Do it! Do it right! Do it right now!

~ Pseudononymous

Visualize

Just imagine yourself enjoying success. Paint the picture in your mind. Go ahead and "count your chickens before they hatch." See the goal. Conceptualize the methods. Execute the plan. Seize the morrow. Have some fun. Enjoy the success. Remember, all good things come to those with patience and who work hard and smart.

~ KTW

Chapter Twenty-seven

Winning Behaviors in Networking

➤ *Do Dynamic Daily Planning*
    Plan your work and work your plan
    Prioritize your objectives
    Set milestones for measurement
    Have a holistic living life model
    ✓ Spiritual
    ✓ Community
    ✓ Family
    ✓ Vocation
    ✓ Self
    Adapt, improvise, and adjust
    Start over if needed

➤ *Make a Networking Commitment*
    Believe in yourself
    Trust your company
    Build value daily
    Know products/services
    Create customers
    Proactively network

➤ *Use Query and Probe in Networking*
    Ask questions
    Listen closely

Find the need
Deliver the goods

➤ *Learn to Handle Disapproval*
Reject refusals
Overcome objections
Accept the decision
Move on to the next

➤ *Practice Preventative Self-Maintenance*
Exercise frequently
Eat properly
Keep healthy relationships
Be true to you

➤ *Engage Lifelong Self-Development*
Read every day
Attend seminars regularly
Listen to educational tapes
Focus on the basics

➤ *Apply the 3A's for Networking Success*
✓ Attitude
✓ Aptitude
✓ Action

Chapter Twenty-eight

Networking Friendships

A *fickle* friend has never seen you cry or known your fears.
A *finest* friend understands and has soggy shoulders from the tears.

A *fickle* friend does not know your parents' first names or look.
A *finest* friend has met them and has their number in an address book.

A *fickle* friend brings a bottle of wine to one of your occasions.
A *finest* friend helps you cook and clean up at the party's cessation.

A *fickle* friend is irritated when you call after they have gone to bed.
A *finest* friend surely asks you why you took so long to call instead.

A *fickle* friend wonders about your past peccadilloes and histories.
A *finest* friend could blackmail you having knowledge of the mysteries.

A *fickle* friend will speak with you about some of your problems.
A *finest* friend listens about your difficulties and helps you solve them.

A *fickle* friend thinks the relationship is over when you simply have an argument.
A *finest* friend knows that a friendship doesn't even begin until after a serious
  disagreement.

A *fickle* friend expects you to always be there just for their need.
A *finest* friend will universally be there for you and will take the lead.

A *fickle* friend will frolic with you up until there is a bend.
A *finest* friend is loyal and will be with you to the journey's end.

A Smile

A smile in the heart,
Is a life-long art.
Transfer to your face,
And it eases the rut and race.
Go forward with joy and delight,
For it comforts the days
And calms the nights.

~ KTW

CHAPTER TWENTY-NINE

Networking Alphabet

*A*void negative people, places, and things. Just be positive.

*B*elieve in yourself, the family, mankind, and your God.

*C*onsider things from every possible point of view.

*D*on't give up and don't give in. Know the difference.

*E*njoy life today. Yesterday is gone. Tomorrow is tomorrow.

*F*amily and friends are treasures. Seek and enjoy their riches.

*G*ive more than you planned to give and take less than given.

*H*old onto all of your dreams and then realize them.

*I*gnore those who try to discourage. Encourage others.

*J*ust do it! But do it right. And do it right now.

*K*eep on trying. No matter how hard it seems, it will get easier.

*L*ove yourself first and foremost. Be your own person.

*M*ake it happen. If it is to be, it is up to me.

*N*ever lie, cheat, or steal. Always strike a fair deal.

*O*pen your eyes and see things as they really are.

*P*ractice makes perfect and perfection takes practice.

*Q*uitters never win, and winners never quit.

*R*ead, study, and learn about everything important in your life.

*S*top procrastinating and start to finish.

*T*ake control of your own destiny. You really do own it.

*U*nderstand yourself in order to better understand others.

*V*isualize it and see it through. Do the next thing first.

*W*ant it more than anything. You can plant a dream.

X-celerate your efforts for results. Results, not effort count.

*Y*ou are unique. In all creation, nothing can replace you.

*Z*ero in on your target! Plan the work and work the plan.

CHAPTER THIRTY

Zing~Zest of Networking

We have the responsibility to wake up each day with a real zest for living life. Daily we need to put the zing in the zest. We have the duty to productively and happily fulfill all of our days. It is our job to seize each moment and make the memories. The critical daily choices for all time are ours to make. Make them well. Here are some of your choices to choose.

♦ Today, I can go to work at the gold mines to dig for gold or the coal mines to work for the company store.

♦ Today, I can whine because I have to go to work, or I can shout for joy because I have a job to do worth doing.

♦ Today, I can complain because I have to go for schooling, or I can eagerly open my mind and fill it with knowledge.

♦ Today, I can murmur about housework, or I can feel good because I have been provided a house as shelter.

♦ Today, I can complain because it is raining, or I can be thankful that the grass is getting greener.

♦ Today, I can grumble about my aches and pains, or I can rejoice that I am alive.

♦ Today, I can be depressed over not having enough money, or I can be encouraged that limitations force me to spend wisely.

♦ Today, I can cry because roses have thorns, or I can celebrate that thorns have roses.

♦ Today, I can lament over what my parents didn't give me growing up, or I can feel grateful that they allowed me to be born.

♦ Today, I can mourn my lack of friends, or I can excitedly embark upon a quest to discover new friendships.

Today stretches ahead of me, waiting to be shaped. Here I am, the sculptor who gets to do the shaping. What today will be like is up to me. I get to choose what kind of day I will have. I will make it GREAT and GRAND!

When the "you" matures, the "does" improve. Your competence goes up in direct proportion to your confidence. Therefore, elevate your personal self-image for positive proficiency.

~ KTW

CHAPTER THIRTY-ONE

Living Life Vicissitudes

Know the dynamics of your whole life with all of its respite and strife.
For some entitled victims proficiently play the game of blame.
Letting go and moving on is the only correct daily fight.
To adapt, adjust, alter, and accommodate change is your fame.

Swerving, shifting, and shuffling are the true adventure.
Permanence and perpetuation is really an earthly perversion.
Always be mindful of the fallible future as we fully mature.
Don't let the "rat run the race" is the accurate interpretation.

We astutely manage the present and then acutely lead into the future.
Being uncomfortable with uncertainty, but unafraid of your venture-vision.
Holding on plainly to the past is more than gross human torture.
Embracing change and seizing tomorrow is your proper mission.

Life's elaborate labyrinth is an intricate and involved maze of haze.
Too many corridors, chambers, curves, and corners abound-around.
Dead-ends and blind spots, going place-to-place can often craze.
Which way? Move or stay! Stop and go! Speed-up or simply slow down.

Today, go forth and fully explore a fresh and novel person, thing, or place.

Be excited about what the vagaries and anomalies might hold.

Have and hold jest and joy in the soul and a warm smile on your face.

You know that the next day will be brand new while yesterday is alone, cold, and old.

Move on to a dissimilar way and a diverse mode of thinking.

Stretch the mind to extended heights and widths with creative concepts.

Keep moving to an improved and more productive orbit of acting.

Coach and challenge yourself to perfect and practice people-pleasing precepts.

Human beliefs, bias, being, and bases are life's locomotions.

Leading nowhere, somewhere, forward, sideways, backwards with little or big commotion.

Routes, returns, and routines are known as the comfortable conditions.

Secure, suitable, safe, and sound are no doubt the favorite positions.

Here comes the unexpected that alters the scheme with great surprise.

A well-being snug and soft milieu is now devastated by the disposition.

This should not be happening, with anger and angst, you sorely and sourly surmise.

Modify, vary, twist, and turn are not part of your special life station.

Oh, those lessons to learn in life so we can avoid any and all psyche and physical mar-jar.

Everyone can search far and wide for their static situation all over the range.

Here and there, near and far, in and out, up and down, or wherever you are.

However, be it understood that there is nothing more constant in life than change.

An acorn to ash is for certain as all creatures and creation will tumble and crumble.

The whole had a beginning and every little bit of thing has an end.

Thus, appreciating our fragile existence through all of life's fumbles and stumbles.

Being neither passive nor apathetic but proactively peaceful before the final ascend.

CHAPTER THIRTY-TWO

Simple Say-Saw Sagacity

A chip on the shoulder often indicates that there is wood higher up.

ß ঽ

A good thing to remember and a better thing to do, is to work with the construction corps and not the wrecking crew.

ß ঽ

A person who minces his words usually chokes on them.

ß ঽ

A road map will tell you everything you want to know, except how to fold it up again.

ß ঽ

A surefire way to double your money is to fold it in half and put it in your pocket.

ß ঽ

Always anticipate the unintentional consequences of your well-intended actions.

$\wp$ $\wp$

Are you going to work in the gold mine or the coal pit? Simple daily perceptions and attitude can make a big difference in life.

$\wp$ $\wp$

As to angels and demons, always let the angels win.

$\wp$ $\wp$

Attitude is a little thing that makes a big difference. It will determine your success in life.

$\wp$ $\wp$

Business goes where it is wanted and stays where it is appreciated.

$\wp$ $\wp$

Celebrate life's special events and life is a celebrity; if not, life goes by ever so prosaically.

$\wp$ $\wp$

Chance favors competence. The harder and smarter one works, the luckier one gets.

$\wp$ $\wp$

Confabulation is the occupation of the many; whereas, action is the purpose of the few.

Do only what is expected and expect the necessities. Do more than what is expected and expect the luxuries.

Do ordinary things extraordinarily well.

Doing as always done gives as always got.

Don't cry because it is over; smile because it happened.

Don't ever take a fence down until you know why it was put up.

Don't expect what you don't inspect.

Don't waste your time on a person who isn't willing to waste his time on you.

Experience is the name everyone gives to their mistakes.

Failure is the opportunity to begin again more intelligently.

Few burdens are heavy when everybody lifts the load.

Footprints on the sand of time are not made by sitting down.

From acorn to oak, the seed needs the feed to flourish.

Generally, if one puts one's shoulder to the wheel and keeps one's eyes on the target, things work out for the best.

God bless the entrepreneur. They take the risk, do the work, create the jobs and pay the wages.

Happiness is not the absence of conflict, but the ability to cope with it.

He who loses wealth loses much; he who loses a friend loses more; but he who loses courage loses all.

ε ɔ

Horse sense means stable thinking.

ε ɔ

If you don't want anyone to know it, don't do it.

ε ɔ

If you want to Boss the Boss, PRODUCE. Production is Profit and Profit is Power.

ε ɔ

In every difficulty, there is opportunity and in every opportunity, there is difficulty.

ε ɔ

In networking, we get through the hole we give through. It's truly the generosity of "me" that begets the reciprocity of "we."

ε ɔ

It's not the problems in life that matter. It's how you solve the problems that makes the difference.

ε ɔ

It's what you learn after you know it all that really counts.

📵 📴

It is better to keep one's mouth closed and be thought a fool than to open it and remove all doubt.

📵 📴

It is better to wear out than rust out.

📵 📴

It is the shallow brook that babbles.

📵 📴

Keep thy shop and thy shop will keep thee.

📵 📴

Leadership by example is the best example of leadership.

📵 📴

Life is too short to be little.

📵 📴

Make the iron hot by striking it.

📵 📴

Many a person has struck out waiting for a base on balls.

ß ᐰ

Most nightmares disappear once you wake up.

ß ᐰ

Networking minus referrals equals not working.

ß ᐰ

Networking symbiosis is toiling together for equal benefit and mutual advantage.

ß ᐰ

Never cut what you can untie.

ß ᐰ

One person with courage is a majority.

ß ᐰ

People buy people, purchase on trust, don't like being sold, and refer like-minded people.

ß ᐰ

Plan your work and work your plan.

ß ᐰ

Please be yourself; who else is better qualified?

ᛒ ᛩ

Practice makes perfect and perfection takes practice.

ᛒ ᛩ

Some are bent with toil, and some get crooked trying to avoid it.

ᛒ ᛩ

Some carve out a future, while others just whittle away their time.

ᛒ ᛩ

Some people are no good at counting calories, and they have the figures to prove it.

ᛒ ᛩ

Stupidity bears a high cost in business as does not acting with prudence.

ᛒ ᛩ

The COURAGEOUS do not live forever, but the CAUTIOUS do not live at all.

ᛒ ᛩ

The difference between motivation and manipulation is all in the motive of the mover.

ᛒ ᛩ

The differential between goodness and greatness is infinitesimal, but the effort is infinite.

ʕ ʔ

The eyes believe themselves. The ears believe other people.

ʕ ʔ

The GAP between knowing "a little bit" and knowing "very little" is a lot!

ʕ ʔ

The lack of planning on *your* part does not justify an emergency on *my* part.

ʕ ʔ

The only dumb question is the one unasked. The dumber question is the one unanswered. The dumbest question of all is the one unasked and unanswered.

ʕ ʔ

The secret of a happy life is not to do what you like, but to like what you do.

ʕ ʔ

There is nothing wrong with making mistakes. Just don't respond with encores.

ʕ ʔ

What is impossible to open is a closed mind.

ʕ ʔ

What is the purpose of material things if there is no one to share them with?

ℬ ℛ

What we have here is a Chinese crisis, for we have both danger and opportunity in the situation.

ℬ ℛ

Whatever you make, make it good and make it happen!

ℬ ℛ

When two people in a business always agree, one of them is unnecessary.

ℬ ℛ

When you do a good job, only great things happen. Make it happen!

ℬ ℛ

Who is rich, asked the child? The contented, humble and happy person, answered Pooh-Bah.

ℬ ℛ

Winners have a practice of doing the things losers don't do.

ℬ ℛ

You can judge a person by how he treats someone who can do nothing for him.

ℬ ℛ

Chapter Thirty-three

Networking Words and Terms

Alter-all ~ a state of mind outside the ego or oneself. This is an advance condition in networking in which we plug others to pitch ourselves. This is a manner of being where the focus of activity is away from ourselves and placed on to others.

B2B ~ commerce between two businesses as in vendor and client.

B2C ~ trade or economic activity that is between an individual consumer and a particular commercial business.

Bigfoot ~ this large manlike creature is said to dwell in the hills and mountains of the wilderness. This android is often described as being covered with hair and standing 8 to 9 feet tall. Legends of the Bigfoot have been around for centuries.

Cans ~ a container; know-how and how-to ability; an expression of the idea of "*YES*" I can.

Can't ~ cannot; can not be done; the opposite of yes; used to deny, refuse, or disagree; nix; negative.

Cascading Effect ~ a massive productive outcome brought about by the aggregate impact of a minute series of interconnected inputs.

Circle of Influence ~ the realm or sphere of sway in which someone acts or exerts power, prestige, prominence, and prerogative.

Conversation Catechisms ~ the teachings of the fundamentals of networking conversations. They are: who, what, where, how, when, and why of query and probe and listen and learn when meeting and greeting people.

Co-op Advertising ~ the practice where two or more networkers jointly market or promote their product/service.

Cost-Benefit ~ a study designed to compare the benefits of a decision to associated costs.

COWABUNGA ~ that product/service feature or characteristic that generates a sufficient level of attention, interest, desire, and action to effect a positive marketing outcome.

Dutch Connection ~ this happens when two networkers meet for a business breakfast, lunch, or dinner (coffee or drinks) to spend some informal time getting acquainted. Each person pays for his/her own fare.

Eeyore ~ an event of "ee" or "or." It is the entity identification method used in the act of giving or receiving something. See rejectee and rejector.

Epitaph ~ a short composition in prose or verse, written as a tribute to a deceased person.

Five "C's" ~ connection, consultation, commentary, construction, and commitment.

FUBAR ~ fouled-up beyond all recognition. A stressful, anxious, agitated, and apprehensive state of affairs caused by mistake, confusion, wrongdoing, depression, and/or fear.

Gargantuan ~ of great size; comprehensive and far-reaching; operating on a big scale; in a large way; enormous, huge, and immense.

Generosity ~ the quality of being generous, willingness to give, unselfishness.

Holistic ~ of or relating to holism; of, concerned with, or dealing with wholes or integrated systems rather than with their parts (Holistic wellness or care).

Inculcate ~ to impress upon the mind by frequent repetition and persistent urging.

IRU~RME ~ an acronym symbolizing the manifestation of symbiotic-synergy. It stands for introduction, recognition, understanding, referring, motivation, and equity.

Kalif ~ Caliph or Kaliph; supreme ruler; dictator or king; secular and religious heads of Islam.

Karmic ~ from the word karma, meaning fate and fortune.

Karmic~the~Wise ~ the king of connectivity; swami of sagacity; majestic marvel; noble knight of nexus; imperial wizard; august potentate; outstanding overlord; great one; sagacious one; wise one of affinity; supreme pontiff; the wise one.

KISS ~ keep it simple and straightforward.

Knots ~ an arrangement of strands; a problem, difficulty, or entanglement; a particle of negation or word expressing the idea of *"NO,"* I can't.

Lagniappe ~ from Creole meaning something extra as in a special gift, gratuity, or tip. The followers of the swami of sagacity used the moniker to denote the networking tips and gifts passed down from *Karmic~the~Wise,* i.e., the book of gifts.

Land of Nothingness ~ a realm of nonexistence; lack of value or worth; uselessness, emptiness, insignificance.

Loyalty Commitment ~ a manifestation of one's depth and breadth in networking.

Luck ~ the seemingly chance happening of events that bring good fortune to someone; luck is what happens when preparation, perspiration, and possibility converge.

Marvelous Miracle ~ the most favorable unexpected consequence of a well-intended action.

Mass Marketing ~ an approach to sales and networking that attempts to reach a broad consumer or networker base, rather than targeting a particular market segment.

Mees ~ the ego; the self.

MOJO ~ that certain personal attribute(s) that gives you some particular charm and positive character that people enjoy, trust, and respect.

Network ~ any arrangement of interconnected or cooperating individuals coming together to develop contacts or exchange information to further their personal and professional lives.

Networking ~ the state of fellowship having common personal and profession interests and purposes. In networking, we create personal friendships and professional relationships. The purpose of networking is to develop symbiotic relationships producing synergistic rewards.

Networking Golden Rule ~ GET *equals* GIVE!

Networking Serendipity ~ being in the right place at the right time through smart and hard networking.

Networking Trifecta ~ creating connections, developing relationships, and building trust. For connections beget connections, relationships beget relationships, trust begets trust, and so on and so on.

NPO ~ a non-profit organization like the Salvation Army, United Way, and American Red Cross.

O'brane ~ a universalistic view of networking where the activity is omnipresent or ubiquitous.

Omnipresent ~ present in all places at the same time.

On-Site Visit ~ the activity where networkers exchange visits to their respective places of business. The function fosters a better understanding of what people do, awareness of the product/service they sell, and deeper appreciation for fellow networkers.

Paradox ~ a statement that seems contradictory, unbelievable, or absurd but that may be true in fact.

Pooh-Bah ~ an important and influential person. An individual whose actions and opinions strongly influence the course of events.

PQS ~ the value formula. To build a success-based business, one must deliver value to the marketplace.

PR ~ (public relations) communications with the general public as through publicity; those functions of an entity concerned with attempting to create favorable public opinion for itself.

Price ~ (1) *Archaic:* value, worth (2) the quantity of one thing that is exchanged or demanded in barter or sale for another (3) the amount of money given or set as consideration for the sale of a specified thing (4) the terms for the sake of which something is done or undertaken (5) the cost at which something is obtained (6) something which one ordinarily accepts in exchange for something else (7) amount which a prospective seller indicates as the sum for which they are willing to sell a good or service.

Proposition ~ a subject or statement to be discussed or debated.

Proposition of the "9-Ps" ~ the core basics of the networking process.

Quality ~ (1) peculiar and essential character, an inherent feature (2) the degree of excellence which a thing possesses, grade; a superiority in kind (merchandise or service of *quality)* (3) distinguishing traits and characteristics consistently promised and achieved (possesses many fine *qualities)* (4) a critical standard of workmanship backed by a mutual pact between the craftsman and their customers (5) marked by zealous adherence to certain features, hallmarks, or specifications.

Reciprocity ~ mutual exchange, especially of leads, business and referrals between two networkers to the advantage of both, whether profit or personal.

Rejectee ~ the one who has been rejected or rebuffed.

Rejector ~ the one who rejects or denies acceptance to another.

ROI ~ the tangible or intangible return (what is received) on an investment (what is given). It is the ratio of cash earnings from any time and/or money that may have been invested.

*Round-Robin*s ~ a procedure in networking where participants in a gathering take turns giving their 30-60-90 second commercial.

Service ~ (1) the occupation or function of serving; employment as a servant (2) the work done to assist or benefit another; contribution to the welfare of others; disposal for use (3) providing ease, advantage, comfort or profit to a patron or friend (4) thoughtful and continuous regard for the current and future well-being of a customer (5) marked by diligence, empathy, candor, constancy, and sincere concern (6) useful labor that does not produce a tangible commodity.

SMO ~ a special marketing offer is a distinctive value that can arouse people to buy a product or service.

Stakeholder ~ a person having a significant share or vested interest in a networking group or commercial business venture.

Sweat Equity ~ the in-kind hard and smart work invested into an endeavor so as to help achieve its mission.

Sweet Equity ~ the investment of cash or tangible liquid assets into an enterprise for "seed" money purposes.

Symbiosis ~ a similar relationship of mutual interdependence.

Synergism ~ a combined or cooperative action or force.

Target Marketing ~ choosing a specific sales audience and developing a relationship, based on defined needs and preferences, with that market.

TIPs Group ~ a number of persons gathered closely together and forming a recognizable unit for the mutual exchange of leads, business, and referrals. It can also be called a leads group or referral group. It is said that we give business tips, i.e., a suggestion, hint, warning, leads, business, or referrals.

Tuit ~ to incite or impel; to urge to action; stir up; rouse; to push, drive, or move; propel.

U'brane ~ a utilitarian perceptive of networking where the work is more selective and specifically useful.

Ubiquitous ~ present, or seeming to be present, everywhere at the same time; omnipresent.

USP ~ a unique selling proposition that has some remarkable trade appeal inciting people to purchase.

Utility ~ something useful; the quality or property of being useful; used in a number of ways.

Value ~ (1) the full measure of price, quality, and service (2) the monetary worth of something; marketable price (3) the characteristic of a product or service which induces people to sacrifice some portion of their purchasing power (past, present, or future) in order to obtain it (4) the process of meeting the customer's primal desire for paying the lowest affordable PRICE to purchase the highest obtainable QUALITY of something that is supported by the best available SERVICE. Value is gratuitous. It is not an endowment, but it is gratis. What is costly to the enterprise are all the actions that do not add value.

Vicissitudes ~ a condition of constant change or alternation, as a natural process; unpredictable changes or variations that keep occurring in life.

Wave-maker ~ a person who *makes* things happen; one with positive pro-action and energy.

Wave-rider ~ a person who *lets* things happen; one with a high degree of apathy and sloth in their actions.

Wealth ~ Goods or services having economic utility; riches; great amount of worldly possessions.

Wees ~ you and others or another; you and I, he and I, she and I, they and I and us.

Wisdom ~ the quality of being wise; power of judging rightly and following the soundest course of action, based on knowledge, erudition, experience, and understanding; sagacity.

Wise ~ having good judgment and prudence; being informed, learned and/or erudite; showing sagacious, judicious, and sound actions.

Work Wonk ~ A person who is slavishly devoted to the pursuit of providing value in networking.

WOWpower ~ the extreme positive energy caused by the conflux of the COW-ABUNGA and MOJO.

If you don't seize the day, the day will seize you.

~KTW

CHAPTER THIRTY-FOUR

Simply Some Sure-Fire Stuff

Here is an informative bibliography of sales and marketing websites that may offer great tips for selling, marketing, and networking.

- http://www.achieveglobal.com
- http://www.bepossettive.com
- http://www.bepowerful.net
- http://www.billbartmann.com
- http://www.briantracyinternational.com
- http://www.businessballs.com
- http://www.characterofexcellence.com
- http://www.confiencecenter.com
- http://www.entrepreneur.com
- http://www.getmoreleads.net
- http://www.gitomer.com
- http://www.gmarketing.com
- http://www.heavyhitterselling.com
- http://www.instantreferralsystem.com
- http://www.justsell.com
- http://www.marketingprofs.com
- http://www.morebusiness.com
- http://www.nevercoldcall.com
- http://www.salestrainingplus.com
- http://www.selfgrowth.com

- http://www.sellingpower.com
- http://www.sharkmasterjr.com
- http://www.tomhopkins.com

This is simply some sure-fire stuff. SURF, READ and ENJOY!

Each person has certain personal choices to choose in living life: They can approach it as a creator or a critic, a lover or a hater, a positive or a negative, or a giver or a taker. It is their choice to choose.

~KTW

CHAPTER THIRTY-FIVE

The Round Tuit

Round Tuit

The Round Tuit was an invention of *Karmic~the~Wise*. It was used by the ancient one to get people focused on getting things done. This valuable tool was lost in the sands of time. But now at long last, we have found a sufficient supply of Round Tuits for each reader to have one of their very own. Guard it with your life. These tuits have been hard to come by, especially the round ones. This tool is an indispensable item in life. Whether you are at home or at work, this Round Tuit will help you become a more efficient and effective person. For years, everyone has heard people say…*"I'll do this or that as soon as I get a round tuit."* Now that you have a Round Tuit of your very own, many~many things which needed to be accomplished will finally get done.

Round Tuit

Just Do It With Your Tuit!

NETWORK

Cans and Knots

Generally, there are two kinds of people in the world. These are the "cans" and the "knots." The "knots" will fully explain why you can't do what needs or ought to be done. They tie everyone in "knots" with their negative attitude. On the other hand, you have the "cans." They will deduce what is at the heart of the problem or what you are trying to do. Then, they will go ahead and figure out a way that it can be done. We have no end of people explaining chapter and verse of why we can't accomplish the endeavor. What we need are more people to show us how we can fulfill and finish the enterprise. These "cans" help society grow and prosper because success only comes in "cans" and not "knots." The "cans" can just because they believe they can. And those who say it can't be done had better get out of the way of those who are going to do it. For in the final analysis, I CAN is more critical than IQ!

~ KTW

☒☒

Part V ~ The Finis

Maybe God wants us to meet a few wrong people before we meet some right ones so when we finally do meet the right people, we will recognize them and be grateful.

~ KTW

The Greatest Game

Oh LIFE, the greatest game. In it, you can choose to be a player or spectator. You can actively participate or simply observe. You can be in the actual fray or just sit on the sidelines. It is your choice to choose. Oh LIFE, it's grand! And, when you think about life, the alternative is deadly. Oh YOU, get in the game.

~ KTW

જી ટ

SUMMARY

Networking can be positively productive. Of course, it must be hardily engaged with intelligence. The first essential is to know what you are trying to accomplish. What industry segments best meet your specific needs and preferences? That is, are you an O'brane or U'brane? Secondly, an effective networker must be willing to move from the status of "me" to the state of "we." *Karmic~the~Wise* once said of commercial business affairs…"We have no eternal customers; we have no eternal competitors; we only have eternal self-interests." In networking matters, the wise one of affinity felt that we must transcend this myopic viewpoint. Thus, true networkers must be ready, willing, and able to make the loyalty commitment. The third essential is to learn about and understand the basics of the networking process. It is a self-taught discipline. Therefore, you will need to do it yourself for yourself through reading, study, practice, and observation. The fourth essential is to inculcate the mechanics. And, finally, you must properly practice the rules of engagement. If you don't, you will become frustrated and fail in some degree or another. If you do, networking will be fun and profitable. It is your choice. As *Karmic~the~Wise* once said…"Work smartly and act wisely."

Richard Possett

CONCLUSION

The end or the last part is where we form an opinion on any literary work. If it is a bad book, readers may never get to the end. They will rush head-on to the conclusion if it is a good publication. Personally, I have read quite a few books in my life, and it still amazes me that the author writes the outcome. They opine on the quality of the composition. What a deal!

Oh my gosh, no doubt the creator will think, no believe, that their particular piece of work is pure literary genius. I believe this is a good, no great, tome and I appreciate your purchase. Furthermore, I know if you properly apply the knowledge in the book, you will be a better networker. I guarantee it!

For **Gargantuan Networking**, I am going to let the reader write the conclusion. Email me at richard@bepossettive.com and give me the straight dope, nitty-gritty, and the gospel truth. I have no fear, so let me know the good, the bad, and the ugly. Again, thank you for reading **Gargantuan Networking**. Have a great day and a better tomorrow. Be super good, but get better. Happy net-working! Say goodnight, Gracie. Goodnight, Gracie.

Richard Possett

EPILOGUE

For many decades, *Karmic~the~Wise* walked about, magically on his trusty carpet, the South Asia market, successfully employing the practices of **Gargantuan Networking**. He was forever busy and, consequently, never formally codified these profitable customs and habits. The profound prophet of networking was always willing to share his ideas. There was always time in his schedule to happily help someone to better understand the way. From person-to-person, his dogma was verbally passed and exponentially applied throughout The Orient. Everyone who could comprehend and carry out the concepts prospered.

In the centuries that followed, more and more of his disciples gainfully embraced the doctrine. They adopted the tenets, even though they were based upon an enormous effort, because it was an interchange of vast wealth. This sharing of riches came in the form of personal and business referrals willfully given and received. This activity was conducted in an environment where the parties enjoyed doing business with one another, for the primary purpose of networking is to happily develop valued business and personal contacts for profit.

Then, at some uncertain time and place, an anonymous group of followers decided to memorialize the traditions of *Karmic~the~Wise* into *The Book of Lagniappe.* This bound volume of networking knowledge became a gift to the ages. For true immortality is but our memory. And, *Karmic~the~Wise* will always be remembered as the original messenger of **Gargantuan Networking**.

ABOUT THE AUTHOR

Richard W. Possett, Sr. is an experienced entrepreneur and seasoned executive from the international financial and insurance services industries. He has successfully used the networking platform for sales and marketing in his various enterprises.

Richard was born and raised in Grand Rapids, Michigan. He lived and worked for five years in Los Angeles, California before moving to Oklahoma. His family has resided in the Tulsa metropolitan area for the last eighteen years.

Richard graduated from Western Michigan University with a BBA degree earning a major in accountancy. He is a CPA, small business owner and operator, lifelong networking practitioner, accredited mortgage loan originator, Financialist, and past SEC-registered securities representative and licensed insurance agent.

Richard is a former international rugby player. He served in the United States Army during the Vietnam War. He has been married to his wife, Marilyn, for more than 41 wonderful years. Richard and Marilyn have three adult children, Nicole, Richard, and Michael; two young grandchildren, Braden and Rebekah; and a terrific son-in-law, Daryl. Richard's hobbies are writing, reading, and walking with his wife and their two golden retrievers.

For a complete catalogue of his literary works please view www.bepossettive.com or to simply contact Richard, please feel free to email him at richard@bepossettive.com. He would like to hear from you.

END NOTE

The character *Karmic~the~Wise* is a sole invention of the author. Any resemblance of a past or present entity in the known universe will be a flabbergasting coincidence. *The Book of Lagniappe* is a figment of the author's imagination. He would apologize to everyone if anyone took umbrage to its use for the purposes in this book.

Richard Possett

INDEX

Suggested Reading

BIADASZ, PETER. *More Leads ~ The Complete Handbook for TIPs Groups, Leads Groups and Networking Groups.* Lincoln, Nebraska: iUniverse, 2005.

BIADASZ, PETER & POSSETT, RICHARD. *Powerful People Are Powerful Networkers ~ Your Daily Guide to Becoming a Powerful Person.* Lincoln, Nebraska: iUniverse, 2006.

CARNEGIE, DALE. *How to Win Friends and Influence People.* New York, New York: Simon & Schuster, 1936.

GOTIMER, JEFFERY. *Little Red Book of Selling.* Austin, Texas: Bard Press, 2004.

HILL, NAPOLEON. *Think and Grow Rich.* New York, New York: Ballantine Books, 1937.

MCKAY, HARVEY. *Dig Your Well Before You're Thirsty~The <u>Only</u> Networking Book You'll Ever Need.* New York, New York: Random House Publishing, 1999.

SMITH, CARRIE PERRIEN. *Networking Zone ~ The Business Referral Network Construction Guide.* Rogers, Arkansas: You Gotta Believe Publishing, 2004.

978-0-595-38778-6
0-595-38778-0